Gotta  ™
Minute

50 TIPS

for organizing your life

by Irene Lawrence

Robert D. Reed Publishers • San Francisco, California

Robert D. Reed Publishers
750 La Playa Street, Suite 647
San Francisco, CA 94121
Phone: 650/994-6570 • Fax: 994-6579
E-mail: 4bobreed@msn.com
Website: www.rdrpublishers.com

Typesetters: Katherine Hyde & Pamela D. Jacobs, M.A.
Book Cover: Julia Gaskill at Graphics Plus, Pacifica, CA

ISBN 1-885003-53-6

Manufactured, Typeset, and Printed in the United States of America

To anyone who feels

discombobulated, overwhelmed,

and organizationally-challenged!

I understand . . . and offer hope.

What is Organizing?

Organizing means: "1 to provide with an organic structure; esp., a) to arrange things in an orderly way; b) to make into a whole with unified and coherent relationships; c) to make plans or to arrange for; 2 to bring into being; establish . . . 4 to set (oneself) into an orderly state of mind . . . ." according to *Webster's New World Dictionary, Third College Edition*, New York: Simon & Schuster, Inc., 1988.

The ABC's of effective organizing* involve:

Accessibility   Having things readily available.

Blending   Assembling similar things together to make the parts more uniform.

Convenience   Having things within easy reach.

Design   Forming a strategy and a plan.

Economizing   Using material resources carefully.

Function   Serving a useful purpose.

Groundwork   Creating a solid foundation.

Harmonizing   Arranging things in a unified way.

Integrating   Making into a whole by joining a system of parts.

Joining   Bringing things together in a unified manner.

Know-how   Using ability and technical skill.

Liquidation   Eliminating unnecessary things.

* Definitions are loosely based on *Webster's New World Dictionary, Third College Edition*, New York: Simon & Schuster, 1988 and *Roget's II The New Thesaurus*, New York: Houghton Mifflin Company, 1995.

Method	Arranging and designing things systematically.
Numeration	Noting of items one by one.
Orderliness	Arranging things systematically.
Prioritizing	Arranging in order of importance.
Quality control	Maintaining desired standards.
Reduction	Condensing and decreasing clutter.
Sorting	Distributing into specific categories.
Transformation	Changing the form or outward appearance of something or someone.
Unity	Assembling together in harmony.
Vision	Forming mental images of a desired outcome.
Workability	Feasibility. Capable of being done.
X	Marking with an "x" and getting rid of excess baggage and clutter.
Yield	Letting go of unnecessary things. Surrendering.
Zeal	Working with enthusiasm.

About This Book

There are lots of books on the shelves clamoring to help you get organized. Maybe you've looked at some of them and thought, "I'm so disorganized, I don't even have time to read one of these books on how to get organized!"

Well, now there's an organization book just for you! This little book offers you 50 quick tips—and we do mean quick!—just to get you thinking about what you need to do to get organized in your own unique situation. We've even given you a blank Action Plan with each tip, where you can jot down your ideas.

So let's get started, and have some fun getting organized!

My Action Plan

PLAN
AHEAD

My Action Plan

Set Goals
for Yourself

My Action Plan

MAKE
LISTS

My Action Plan

4

Keep a
Calendar

1

My Action Plan

COLOR CODE

My Action Plan

6

Keep It
Simple

My Action Plan

Establish a
Routine

My Action Plan

Throw away any unnecessary items

My Action Plan

USE
LABELS

My Stuff

My Action Plan

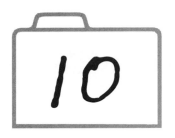

Keep a Schedule

My Action Plan

USE CONTAINERS

My Action Plan

12

Be Well
Informed

My Action Plan

Be
Flexible

My Action Plan

Use Color
Pens

My Action Plan

15

Smile

My Action Plan

Categorize
Similar Items

My Action Plan

BE RESPONSIBLE

My Action Plan

36

18

Make a Budget for Yourself

My Action Plan

19

Be
Timely

My Action Plan

USE
MARKERS

My Action Plan

Be
Resourceful

My Action Plan

USE BOXES FOR STORAGE

My Action Plan

23

Be Neat and Orderly

My Action Plan

24

Keep a Diary of Special Events

My Action Plan

25

USE
FOLDERS

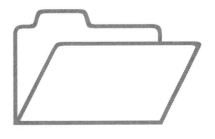

My Action Plan

Alphabetize
Your Folders

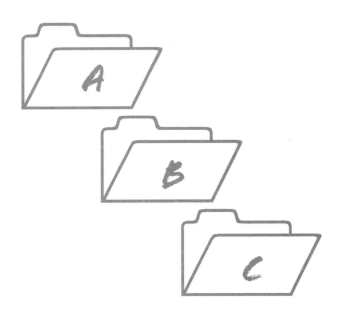

My Action Plan

27

Reward Yourself for a Job Well Done

My Action Plan

Recognize What
Works for You

My Action Plan

29

Have pen and paper
at your fingertips
to jot down
your great ideas
when they come
to you

My Action Plan

30

Take advantage of
sales on products
you are in the
market for

My Action Plan

Use Your
Imagination

My Action Plan

32

Make Yourself a Follow-up Folder

My Action Plan

33

Take One Step at a Time

My Action Plan

34

Know exactly
how much money
you have in your
checking/savings
accounts and all
other investments
at all times

My Action Plan

35

Chart your
spending and
savings on a
monthly basis

My Action Plan

36

USE COLORED PENCILS

My Action Plan

37

Follow Through on Projects

My Action Plan

38

Clip out coupons
ONLY
for products
you use

My Action Plan

39

EAT HEALTHFULLY

My Action Plan

40

Exercise

My Action Plan

Focus on What You Want Done

My Action Plan

Be Humble

My Action Plan

43

Don't
Procrastinate

My Action Plan

Be
Patient

My Action Plan

ACCEPT CHANGE

My Action Plan

Be Open-
Minded

My Action Plan

47

Set aside a quiet
fifteen minutes
to collect
your thoughts

My Action Plan

48

Keep commonly used phone numbers at your fingertips

My Action Plan

Use a
Photo
Album

My Action Plan

Use a scrapbook

Books Available From Robert D. Reed Publishers

Please include payment with orders. Send indicated book/s to:

Name:_____

Address:_____

City:_____ State:_____ Zip:_____

Phone:(_____)_____ E-mail:_____

<table>
<tr><td><u>Titles and Authors</u></td><td>Unit
Price</td></tr>
<tr><td>Gotta Minute? 50 Tips for Organizing Your Life!
by Irene Lawrence</td><td>$7.95</td></tr>
<tr><td>Gotta Minute? Practical Tips for Abundant Living:
The ABC's of Total Health by Tom Massey, Ph.D., N.D.</td><td>9.95</td></tr>
<tr><td>Gotta Minute? Yoga for Health, Relaxation &
Well-being by Nirvair Singh Khalsa</td><td>9.95</td></tr>
<tr><td>Gotta Minute? How to Look and Feel Great!
by Marcia F. Kamph, M.S., D.C.</td><td>11.95</td></tr>
<tr><td>Gotta Minute? Ultimate Guide of One-Minute
Workouts for Anyone, Anywhere, Anytime!
by Bonnie Nygard, M.Ed. & Bonnie Hopper, M.Ed.</td><td>9.95</td></tr>
<tr><td>A Kid's Herb Book For Children Of All Ages
by Lesley Tierra, Acupuncturist and Herbalist</td><td>19.95</td></tr>
<tr><td>Saving The Soul of Medicine by M. A. Mahony, M.D.</td><td>21.95</td></tr>
<tr><td>House Calls: How we can all heal the world
one visit at a time by Patch Adams, M.D.</td><td>11.95</td></tr>
<tr><td>500 Tips For Coping With Chronic Illness
by Pamela D. Jacobs, M.A.</td><td>11.95</td></tr>
</table>

Enclose a photocopy of this order form with payment for books. Send to the address below. Shipping & handling: $2.50 for first book plus $1.00 for each additional book. California residents add 8.5% sales tax. We offer discounts for large orders.

Please make checks payable to the publisher: Robert D. Reed. Total enclosed: $_____. See our website for more books!

Robert D. Reed Publishers
750 La Playa, Suite 647, San Francisco, CA 94121
Phone: 650-994-6570 • Fax: 650-994-6579
Email: 4bobreed@msn.com • www.rdrpublishers.com